G000123746

KITCHEN
WISDOM

KITCHEN WISDOM

A Collection of Savory Quotations

Illustrated by Christopher Wormell

Running Press
PHILADELPHIA • LONDON

A Running Press Miniature Edition™

Copyright © 1995 by Running Press. Illustrations copyright © 1994 Christopher Wormell. Printed in China. All rights reserved under the Pan-American and International Copyright Conventions.

Canadian representatives: General Publishing Co., Ltd., 30 Lesmill Road, Don Mills, Ontario M3B 2T6.

Library of Congress Cataloging-in-Publication Number 94-73888

ISBN 1-56138-622-7

This book may be ordered by mail from the publisher. Please add $1.00 for postage and handling.
But try your bookstore first!

Running Press Book Publishers
125 South Twenty-second Street
Philadelphia, Pennsylvania 19103-4399

CONTENTS

Cooking is a creative act that fulfills a yearning—not just to eat, but to savor, to surrender to the pleasure of food. Those who cook offer nourishment, satisfaction, and contentment, no small achievement when

uncertainty often seems to be
the norm of human existence.
The cook who presents a meal in
all of its complex textures and
flavors feeds both body and
soul.

There is an amiable alchemy
in the kitchen. The ingredients
are noble in their simplicity: an
onion with its perfect rings

connected by the wisp of membrane, an egg with its pure shape that speaks of life's beginnings, a leaf of basil with the smell of fertility still clinging to its stem…these are the beginnings. Enter the cook and they are transformed from ordinary to delectable, from inert to aromatic, from earthbound to divine. Suddenly, soufflés rise, sauces thicken, scents intoxicate. To blend ingredients is to find a new essence, to create an enchanted whole that is much more than the sum of its parts.

To spend time in the kitchen is never to be alone, for there is a rich heritage of cooks that came before. Whether in childhood kitchens or in cookbooks, these sage mavens share their memories, their humor, and their accumulated wisdom. Within this volume, celebrate their luscious legacy with an appetizing array of quotations and illustrations.

ART

Cooking is at once one of
the simplest and most
gratifying of the arts, but
to cook well one must
love and respect food.

CRAIG CLAIBORNE
(B. 1920)
AMERICAN FOOD EDITOR
AND WRITER

Non-cooks think it's silly
to invest two hours' work
in two minutes'
enjoyment; but if cooking
is evanescent, well,
so is the ballet.

JULIA CHILD (B. 1912)
AMERICAN CHEF AND WRITER

Kitchens are exciting places.
The four elements of the
ancients (earth, as represented
by the food substances born of

it, water, fire, and air) co-mingle
and re-combine. Sizzling, boil-
ing, activity; the onions as they
sauté, the wash of steam as
the pasta is drained in the sink,
the waft of baking bread, the
pulsing white-veined heart of
the deep purple cabbage, the
transformation from liquid
to solid of the cakes as they

bake—these tasks and rhythms
remain, for me, something both
holy and fun. Cooking has
alchemy and theater, the joy of
creation; the sensual pleasure of
touching and sniffing glorious
foodstuffs; the pleasure of
pleasing others....

CRESCENT DRAGONWAGON
(B. 1952)
AMERICAN WRITER

Cooking…means the knowledge
of all herbs, and fruits, and
balms, and spices; and of all that
is healing and sweet in fields and
groves, and savory in meats;
it means carefulness, and in-
ventiveness, and watchfulness,
and willingness, and readiness of
appliance; it means the economy
of your great-grandmothers and

the science of modern chemists; it means much tasting, and no wasting... it means, in fine...that everybody has something pretty to put on...[and] yet more imperatively, that everybody has something good to eat.

JOHN RUSKIN (1819–1900)
ENGLISH ART CRITIC AND WRITER

It does not matter whether one paints a picture, writes a poem, or carves a statue, simplicity is the mark of a master-hand. Don't run away with the idea that it is easy to cook simply. It requires a long apprenticeship.

ELSIE DE WOLFE
(1865–1950)
AMERICAN DECORATOR
AND WRITER

Baking is just like driving
a car: you can read every
manual you can get your
hands on, but until you
get in and do it, you
won't really learn how.

MARION CUNNINGHAM
20TH-CENTURY AMERICAN CHEF

All cooks are debtors to
history, either gone by or
in the making.

**PETER VAN RENSSELAER
LIVINGSTON
[JAMES TOWNSEND]
(B. 1910)
AMERICAN WRITER**

The bishop smiled
approvingly. "A soup like
this is not the work of
one man," he said, "it is
the result of a constantly
refined tradition.
There are nearly a
thousand years of history
in this soup."

**WILLA CATHER (1876–1947)
AMERICAN WRITER**

Designing hors d'oeuvres
is not different from
designing sets and
costumes. And being nice
to people. Food is very
much theatre.

**JAMES BEARD (1903–1985)
AMERICAN CHEF AND WRITER**

I always plan dinner first
thing in the morning.
That's the only way I can
get through the day,
having a specific meal to
look forward to at night.

ALAN KING
(B. 1927)
AMERICAN ENTERTAINER

It has always seemed strange to me that people can be vague and casual about what they put into their mouths as food and drink.

**PAMELA VANDYKE PRICE
(B. 1923)
ENGLISH WRITER**

Some cook, some do not
cook, some things can
not be altered....

**EZRA POUND (1885–1972)
AMERICAN POET, CRITIC,
AND EDITOR**

Heaven sends us good
meat, but the devil
sends us cooks.

**DAVID GARRICK (1717–1779)
ENGLISH ACTOR, PRODUCER,
AND DRAMATIST**

Cooking is like
matrimony—two things
served together
must match.

**YUAN MEI (1716–1798)
CHINESE POET**

Cooking with love means
never having to feel
chained to your stove,
never feeling that getting
dinner on the table is a
teeth-gritting experience
rather than a
charming interlude.

FRANCIS ANTHONY
20TH-CENTURY AMERICAN CHEF

Hunger is the teacher of
the arts, and the bestower
of invention.

**PERSIUS (34–62 A.D.)
ROMAN SATIRIST**

Like a love affair, a
cookbook is probably
easier to get into than out
of. At the end of both,
sins of commission and
omission loom large.
What was said that had
better been left unsaid?

**PEG BRACKEN (B. 1920)
AMERICAN WRITER**

Chef: Any cook who
swears in French.

HENRY BEARD
AND
ROY MCKIE
20TH-CENTURY AMERICAN
WRITERS

A person who observes
the rules of proper
nutrition is a person who
should never be placed in
charge of a barbecue.

**DAVE BARRY
(B. 1947)
AMERICAN WRITER AND
HUMORIST**

That's the way Chinese
mothers show they love
their children, not
through hugs and kisses
but with stern offerings of
steamed dumplings,
duck's gizzard, and crab.

AMY TAN (B. 1952)
AMERICAN WRITER

Whatever the seasoning,
whatever the dish,
whatever the occasion, do
it generously and with
love, for that in the end is
what the shared
experience of cooking and
eating is all about.

ELIZABETH ROZIN
20TH-CENTURY AMERICAN
WRITER

ELEMENTS

[An herb is] the friend
of physicians and
the praise of cooks.

**CHARLEMAGNE
(742–814)
FRANKISH KING**

If I had to choose just
one plant for the whole
herb garden, I should be
content with basil.

ELIZABETH DAVID
20TH-CENTURY
ENGLISH WRITER

It is not really an
exaggeration to say that
peace and happiness
begin, geographically,
where garlic is used
in cooking.

X. MARCEL BOULESTIN
(1878–1943)
FRENCH CHEF

It is hard to imagine
a civilization
without onions.

**JULIA CHILD (B. 1912)
AMERICAN CHEF AND WRITER**

A pound of dried basil
will season enough
chicken cacciatore to
feed over three
thousand people.

**AMERICAN SPICE TRADE
ASSOCIATION**

Imagine that a fierce pestilence strikes the earth and obliterates forever a single crop—ginger. The consequences would be appalling: no more gingerbread for school kids, no more gingersnaps to dunk into milk and no more ginger ale to soothe upset stomachs. No one would handle a delicate task "gingerly." And lively red-haired women would answer to some other spicy name.

BARBARA HANSEN
(B. 1941)
AMERICAN WRITER

…laughter is the best
seasoning there is.

BARBARA KAFKA (B. 1933)
AMERICAN WRITER

As a cook I was always fascinated with eggs. I saw them as a culinary magic wand, turning thick batters into tall, puffed soufflés and milky liquids into firm custards. The whites were thrilling, the way they jelled and turned opaque as they cooked, or whipped into a stiff white foam.

PHYLLIS C. RICHMAN (B. 1939)
AMERICAN WRITER

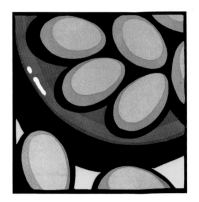

…crabmeat, one of the
world's most delectable
foods…. Crab may be
very close to what the
gods eat if they have
fisherman up there….

JAMES A. MICHENER
(B. 1907)
AMERICAN WRITER

At court, the pea saga
still continues. The desire
to eat them, the pleasure
of having eaten them and
the joy of eating them
again are the three topics
on which our princes
have dwelt for the past
four days. There are
ladies who, after having

dined with the king, and dined well, at home find peas to eat before they go to bed, despite the risk of indigestion. It is a fad, a craze, and the one follows the other.

MADAME DE MAINTENON [FRANÇOISE D' AUBIGNÉ] (1635–1719) FRENCH MARCHIONESS

Two or three people,
when I've prodded them,
have mumbled of apples:
biting into them, feeling
the cold juice flow into
the mouth corners,
hearing the snap of skin
and pulp.

But the spontaneous
revelations are rare. They

must, from what I have
discovered, be inspired by
wine or high emotional
pressure. They are thus
doubly poignant.

**M.F.K. FISHER
(1908–1992)
AMERICAN WRITER**

People who loathe the
idea of a salad are very
like those who claim
not to like perfume:
they just haven't met
the right one.

MIRIAM POLUNIN
20TH-CENTURY AMERICAN
WRITER AND BROADCASTER

I can recommend this dish to all who have confidence in me: salad refreshes without weakening, and comforts without irritating, and I have a habit of saying that it makes us younger.

ANTHELME BRILLAT-SAVARIN (1755–1826) FRENCH WRITER AND POLITICIAN

Sunbeams may be extracted
from cucumbers,
but the process is tedious.

**DAVID DAGGET
(1764–1851)
AMERICAN SENATOR**

Oh, the delicious fruits that
we have here and in Syria!
Orange gardens miles
in extent, citrons,
pomegranates; but the
most delicious thing in the
world is a banana, which
is richer than a pineapple.

**BENJAMIN DISRAELI
(1804–1881)
BRITISH POLITICIAN
AND WRITER**

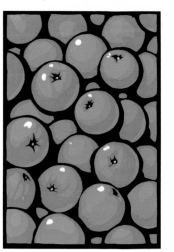

The sweetness of a ripe
guava cannot be
compared to anything
else: its pink, gooey
inside can be held on the
tongue and savored
like a caramel.

JUDITH ORTIZ COFER
(B. 1952)
PUERTO RICAN-born
AMERICAN WRITER

The cherry tomato is a
wonderful invention,
producing, as it does, a
satisfactorily explosive
squish when bitten.

**MISS MANNERS
[JUDITH MARTIN]
(B. 1938)
AMERICAN COLUMNIST**

Asparagus should be sexy
and almost fluid....

**DIANA VREELAND
(1903–1989)
FRENCH-BORN AMERICAN
FASHION EDITOR**

What garlic is to salad,

insanity is to art.

**AUGUSTUS SAINT-GAUDENS
(1848–1907)
IRISH-BORN AMERICAN
SCULPTOR**

Let the sky rain potatoes.

**WILLIAM SHAKESPEARE
(1564–1616)
ENGLISH DRAMATIST AND POET**

Cabbage, n: A familiar kitchen-garden vegetable about as large and wise as a man's head.

**AMBROSE BIERCE
(1842–1914)
AMERICAN WRITER**

There may be as many
good fish in the sea as
ever came out of it,
but cooking them is even
more difficult than
catching them.

**MADELEINE BINGHAM
(B. 1912)
AMERICAN WRITER**

He was a bold man that
first ate an oyster.

**JONATHAN SWIFT
(1667–1745)
ENGLISH WRITER**

...I don't remember any
oysters in...the Midwest I
grew up in, but I have
been trying to make up
for their absence ever
since I left....

CALVIN TRILLIN (B. 1935)
AMERICAN WRITER

History records the battlefields on which we lose our lives…but it cannot tell us the origin of wheat. Such is human folly.

**JEAN-HENRI FABRE
(1823–1915)
FRENCH ENTOMOLOGIST**

There's somebody at
every dinner party who eats
all the celery.

KIN HUBBARD (1868–1930)
AMERICAN HUMORIST AND WRITER

Beautiful Soup, so rich
  and green,
Waiting in a hot tureen!
Who for such dainties
  would not stoop!
Soup of the evening,
  beautiful Soup!

**LEWIS CARROLL
[CHARLES DODGSON]
(1832–1898)
ENGLISH WRITER AND
MATHEMATICIAN**

ALCHEMY

When pleasures to the eye
and palate meet,
That cook has render'd his
great work complete.

MARIA J. MOSS
19TH-CENTURY AMERICAN WRITER

"I believe there is more satisfaction in being a good cook than in being a good writer. When you are a success you know it surely and immediately."

**A CONTEMPORARY NOVELIST,
AS QUOTED BY
VIRGINIA PASLEY
(1905–1986)
AMERICAN JOURNALIST**

Sometimes it is the only worthwhile product you can salvage from a day: what you make to eat…. Cooking therefore, can keep a person who tries sane.

JOHN IRVING
(B. 1942)
AMERICAN WRITER

...a way of cooking
can produce something
that approaches an
aesthetic emotion.

**ALICE B. TOKLAS
(1877–1967)
AMERICAN WRITER**

...there are very few
people who can resist,
deep down, the earthy,

sensual aroma and flavor
of meat, poultry, or fish
gently boiled with or
without vegetables and
flavored with herbs and
spices…. A lusty stew
brings out the primitive
in all of us….

JAMES VILLAS
(B. 1938)
AMERICAN JOURNALIST

Looked at in the right light, any food might be thought aphrodisiac.

**DIANE ACKERMAN (B. 1948)
AMERICAN POET**

Like a weeded and
pruned garden, bread
stands for the triumph of
man's art over chaotic
nature, from the brick
ovens of Pompeii to the
adobe ovens of the
Pueblos and the electric
ovens of Manhattan.

BETTY FUSSELL
(B. 1927)
AMERICAN WRITER

Food imaginatively and
lovingly prepared, and
eaten in good company,
warms the being with
something more than the
mere intake of calories.

**MARJORIE KINNAN RAWLINGS
(1896–1953)
AMERICAN WRITER**

Cook things so you can
tell what they are. Good
plain food ain't
committed no crime an'
don't need no disguise.
Fancified cooks is
the criminals.

**MARY LASSWELL
(1905–1994)
AMERICAN WRITER**

Good food…should not
be regarded as a poison,
a medicine, or a talisman.
It should be eaten
and enjoyed.

**FROM A REPORT OF THE
NATIONAL ACADEMY OF
SCIENCES**

Woe to the cook whose
sauce has no sting.

**GEOFFREY CHAUCER (1342–1400)
ENGLISH POET**

There is no dessert quite
like a baked soufflé!
A good soufflé is like
a bud that has opened
to full bloom!

ROBERT H. SCHULLER
(B. 1926)
AMERICAN CLERIC AND WRITER

Good cooking fattens
a clear conscience.

**DESESSARTS
[DENIS DÉCHANET]
(1738–1793)
FRENCH ACTOR AND
GASTRONOME**

The full use of taste is
an act of genius.

JOHN LA FARGE (1835–1910)
AMERICAN ARTIST

ABOUT THE ILLUSTRATOR

Christopher Wormell is the author and illustrator of the best-selling children's book *An Alphabet of Animals*, winner of the Graphics Prize at the Bologna Book Fair in 1990. A self-taught artist who dropped out of school at age 18 to pursue painting, he began engraving in

1982 and has won worldwide
recognition as an illustrator.
An Alphabet of Animals was
followed by an illustrated
edition of *Mowgli's Brothers*, the
first story of Rudyard Kipling's
The Jungle Book, and *A Number
of Animals*, which was featured
on the *New York Times* list of
books of the year.

This book has been bound using handcraft methods and Smyth-sewn to ensure durability.

The dust jacket and interior were designed by Ken Newbaker.

The text was edited by William King.

The text was set in Bauer Bodoni and Copperplate 33BC.